Growing Up

Dona Herweck Rice

Every living thing **grows up.**

It **changes** as it grows.

It gets bigger.

Sometimes, it gets much bigger!

It gets faster.

Sometimes, it gets much faster!

It may get more hair.

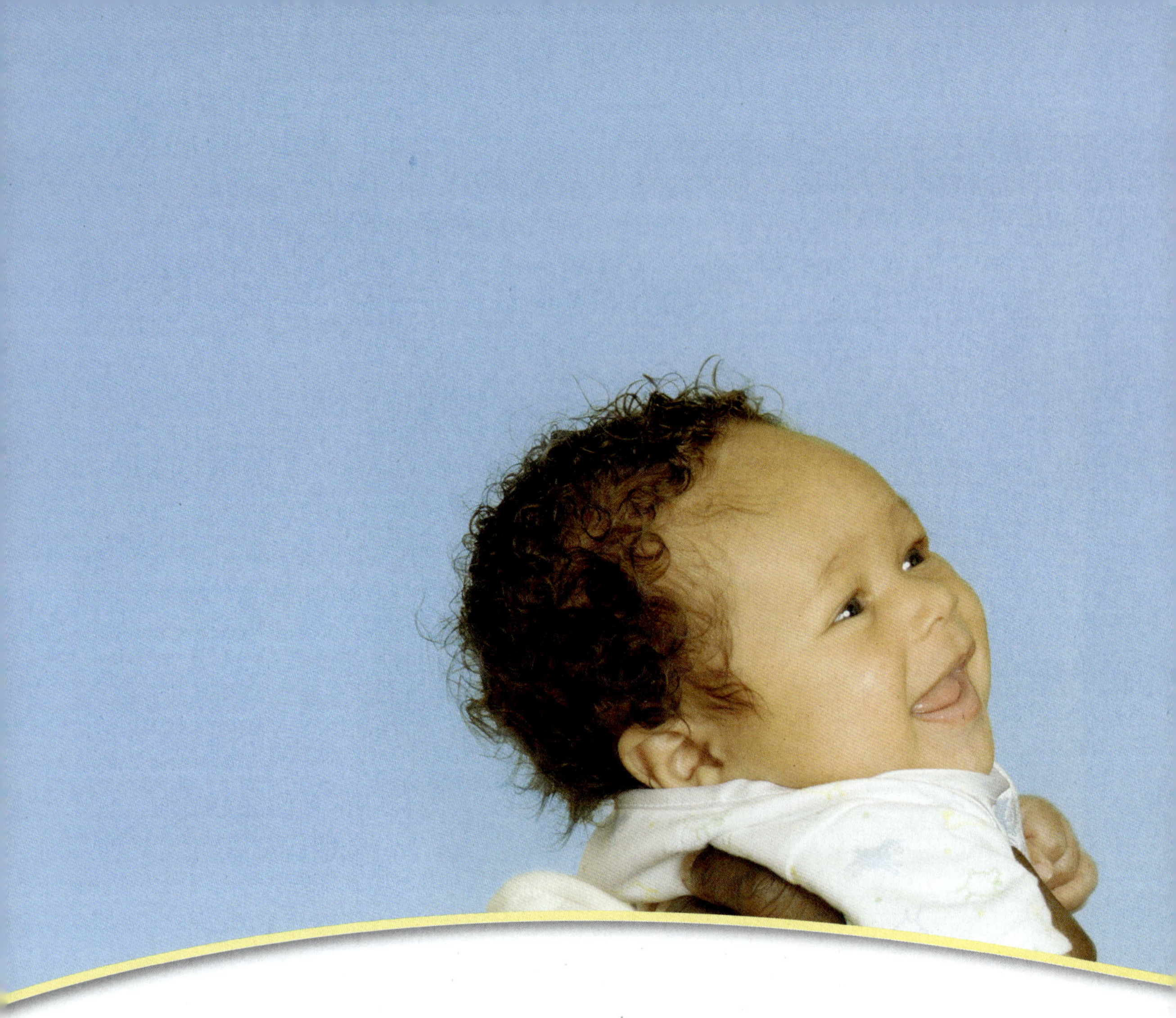

It may get less hair!

It may know more things.

It may do more things.

Change is a big part of growing up.

Let's Do Science!

How do you change over time?
Try this!

What to Get

- ❑ paper and pencil
- ❑ plant
- ❑ tape measure

What to Do

1. Get a calendar.

2. Have an adult help you measure the plant.

3. Write the plant's height on the calendar.

4. Do this each week for a month. At the end of the month, what changed?

Glossary

changes—becomes different in some way

grows up—becomes an adult

Index

Your Turn!

Look at photos of you from the time you were born until now. Draw pictures to show how you have changed.

Consultants

Sally Creel, Ed.D.
Curriculum Consultant

Leann Iacuone, M.A.T., NBCT, ATC
Riverside Unified School District

Jill Tobin
California Teacher of the Year
Semi-Finalist
Burbank Unified School District

Publishing Credits

Conni Medina, M.A.Ed., *Managing Editor*
Lee Aucoin, *Creative Director*
Diana Kenney, M.A.Ed., NBCT, *Senior Editor*
Lynette Tanner, *Editor*
Lexa Hoang, *Designer*
Hillary Dunlap, *Photo Editor*
Rachelle Cracchiolo, M.S.Ed., *Publisher*

Image Credits: Cover & pp.1, 4, 8, 24 iStock; p.9 Richard Kolar/age fotostock; p.22 Cultura Creative/Alamy; p.12 Radius Images/Alamy; p.17 UpperCut Images/Alamy; p.14 Elmar Herz/imagebroker; p.10 Splash News/Newscom; pp.18–19 (illustrations) J.J. Rudisill; all other images from Shutterstock.

Library of Congress Cataloging-in-Publication Data

Rice, Dona, author.
Growing up / Dona Herweck Rice.
pages cm
Summary: "It is time to learn how living things grow and change."—Provided by publisher.
Audience: K to grade 3.
Includes index.
ISBN 978-1-4807-4524-7 (pbk.) —
ISBN 978-1-4807-5133-0 (ebook)
1. Growth--Juvenile literature. 2. Life cycles (Biology)—Juvenile literature. 3. Readers (Primary) I. Title.
QH511.R623 2015
571.8—dc23
2014008924

Teacher Created Materials
5301 Oceanus Drive
Huntington Beach, CA 92649-1030
http://www.tcmpub.com

ISBN 978-1-4807-4524-7

Printed by: 51497
Printed in: China